MW00956091

Little Bible Heroes™
Samson

Written by Victoria Kovacs
Illustrated by David Ryley

B&H KIDS
NASHVILLE, TENNESSEE

GOLDQUILL
WWW.GOLDQUILL.CO.UK

fb.com/littlebibleheroes

Published 2017 by B&H Kids, a division of LifeWay Christian Resources, Nashville, Tennessee.
Text and illustrations copyright © 2017, GoldQuill, United Kingdom.
All rights reserved. Scripture quotations are taken from the Christian Standard Bible ®
Copyright © 2017 by Holman Bible Publishers. Used by permission.
ISBN: 978-1-4627-4338-4   Dewey Decimal Classification: CE
Subject Heading: SAMSON \ GIDEON \ BIBLE STORIES
Printed in February 2021 in Dongguan, Guangdong, China
3 4 5 6 7 8 9 • 25 24 23 22 21

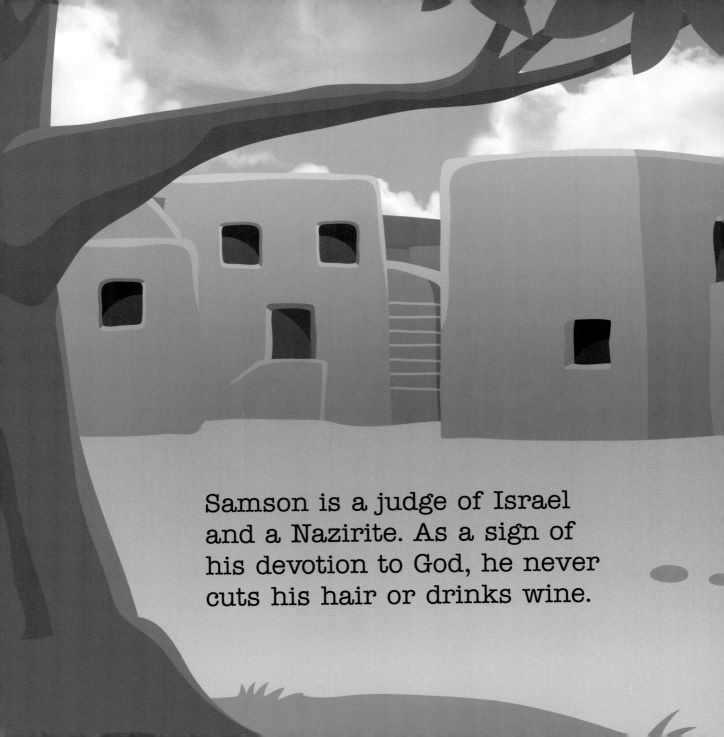

Samson is a judge of Israel and a Nazirite. As a sign of his devotion to God, he never cuts his hair or drinks wine.

One day a young lion roars
at Samson. The Spirit of God
comes on Samson and gives
him strength to defeat the lion.

The Philistines, Israel's enemies, try to arrest Samson, but the Spirit of God comes on him again. He uses a bone to defeat a thousand men.

One night, some men wait to capture Samson at the city gate. Instead he picks up the city gate and carries it to the top of a hill.

The Philistines are angry. They ask a woman named Delilah to trick Samson and find out what makes him strong.

Delilah finds out the secret to Samson's great strength: his hair! While he sleeps, the Philistines shave his head. His strength is gone. They blind him and put him in prison.

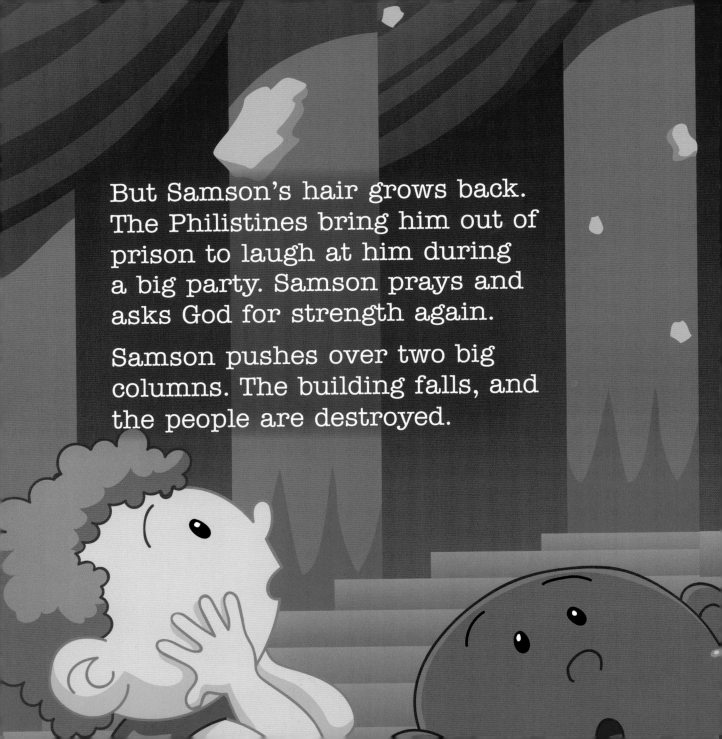

But Samson's hair grows back. The Philistines bring him out of prison to laugh at him during a big party. Samson prays and asks God for strength again.

Samson pushes over two big columns. The building falls, and the people are destroyed.

Read:

You will conceive and give birth to a son. You must never cut his hair, because the boy will be a Nazirite to God from birth, and he will begin to save Israel from the power of the Philistines. —Judges 13:5

Think:

1. Where did Samson get his strength?
2. Samson prayed to God for help. Do you ask God for help?

Remember:

God gives us strength too.

Read:

The land had peace for forty years during the days of Gideon.—Judges 8:28

Think:

1. How did God help Gideon?
2. Do you trust God to help you do brave things?

Remember:

God can make you brave!

"A sword for the LORD and for Gideon!" they shout. The enemy is scared and runs away. God's army wins!

Gideon and his men stand at
the edge of the enemy's camp.
They blow their horns and break
pitchers that hide their torches.

Gideon sneaks near the Midianite camp. He hears a man telling his friend about a strange dream. His friend says the dream means Midian will lose the battle.

God says Gideon still has too many men. Gideon must choose only the ones who use their hands to drink water from the stream. Only three hundred men remain.

It is time to prepare for battle. God says Gideon has too many soldiers. Gideon tells them to go home if they are afraid. Twenty-two thousand men leave.

That night, Gideon secretly
destroys an altar to a false
god. He builds a new altar to
God instead.